OUR STORIES
ATTOCK TO ATTOCK
PARK

Introduction

'Why are our stories not written down? You know, the elder generation is leaving and we will lose our history with them.'

With each member of the first generation of Pakistani immigrants that passes away, there is a sense of panic that we will lose all the knowledge that they held, all the stories that we never asked or penned. What was their home like when they came here? What were the traditions at weddings and funerals in those days? How did they mark Ramzaan and celebrate Eid? Did they face discrimination? What was their journey like to England?

The last time we had this conversation it was at an event about Kashmiri literature and poetry. This time the conversation ended with, 'You teach creative writing? Why can't you gather these stories?' So, we decided even though we can't gather the stories of all of Bradford, we can take a small step.

This book is a result of that small step.

With support from Creative Place Maker, Bradford Moor Pass Team, Volunteers of Attock Park, The Leap and Bradford Council, we set up a weekly Sunday afternoon session in one of the cabins at Attock Park and invited members of an established women's group to join us for ten weeks to share their own stories. Most women came for gardening or a catchup and didn't want to be doing 'work', however, a small number of dedicated women came along regularly and told, wrote and listened to each other's memories on shared themes. Some women only attended one, others every session. All the contributions have been included. The participants varied in age from their teens to their 70s. We saw that as a strength as it didn't just tell the stories of people coming from a range of provinces in Pakistan and Kashmir to England, but additionally, the stories of Bradford Moor residents making the reverse journey and travelling to Pakistan for the first time along with their experiences of growing up in Bradford Moor. These too are our stories, just from a different vantage point.

Pieces have been transcribed, typed up and in some cases translated, with minimal editing to ensure the authentic voice can be heard. For this reason, the home language words used have not been translated and the different spellings used by the participants have been kept, giving a range of ways of spellings the same word such as Ramzaan, Ramadan, as this shows the difference in how these communities pronounce the words.

The book cover photo is one of the name of the park, amongst other artwork displayed at Attock Park

These stories were gathered during the above creative writing sessions and presented as this book by the facilitator, writer and poet, Nabeela Ahmed. Some of the participants are from Attock in Pakistan, the rest are from cities across Pakistan and Kashmir. However, one commonality that they now all share is that they all reside in the area surrounding Attock Park, Bradford.

The participants did not want to share their real names and therefore have chosen pseudonyms for themselves or have asked that only their initials are used.

Acknowledgments

It has been a privilege to gather these stories into this book and I couldn't have done this without on the ground support from the volunteers at Attock Park, who helped set up the first session, brought the refreshments and were on hand throughout the course to ensure it ran smoothly.

Noreen Shah, who opened the cabin each week, assisted with the recruitment of group members and provided on-going support.

Finally, and fundamentally, gratitude must be extended to all the participants who delved into their pasts in order to share their stories and enable this book to be given life.

Contents

School

Windmill Notebook (Bradford, 2010)

You can probably still find it, it's an old relic now but it
still exists
Even now I can picture it clearly, the large A4
notebook
The front and back were the same, bound by spirals
The cover design is embedded in my memory
It was a windmill, no, a water mill.
A windmill watermill then, a building with the fan and
also a water fan by the water
water and trees and windmill/watermill
It's burnt into my memory

It was for Urdu, I'll never forget that
I will never forget being made to sit at the kitchen
table and write
Write the words, learn the words, speak the words
Copy it from exercise books,
You know, those little exercise books with grey dull
pages
and dotted letters and words
All the while my mother stood at my back to make me
stay
and work and not play

I hated it

How I hated that notebook
I hated the words inside
What would I need them for?

They weren't my words.
They were strange, only half familiar because of how
similar they were to what my mother spoke
And also because my mother did sometimes speak it
Also the radio. The radio spoke it.
I hated it all.

Bent over the table for hours I struggled
to write
Head down, pen in hand, I hated
to write
Mum stood over me, trying to force me
to write

I hated it.

This notebook was of words I didn't know
These lessons were of words I didn't want
This whole ordeal was a nightmare I didn't like
This business was nonsense I didn't need

I hated it all.

Eventually, the lessons stopped
The words grew rusty on my tongue
I was being made to learn Arabic
I didn't hate it. I knew it.
Meanwhile the other language
In the other notebook, the water windmill one,
The writing grew faded, the pages stiff
And I didn't open it

I remember it

Sometimes I'll open it
When it's of my own accord
Sometimes I will open it
I'll look at the faded pages
I'll see the messy scrawl of my angry 7 year old self
I can kind of read the faded words

I don't really hate it

Sometimes I'll want to be able to read it better
Sometimes I'll want to be able to speak it
But mostly, I'm not bothered
Sometimes I want to open the notebook again
Sometimes I want to finish the notebook
But mostly, it's not my main concern
I'm choosing to learn Japanese now, after all.
And I enjoy it.

- Liyana Aiza

My School Life, Bradford Moor

I remember my mum leaving me crying at the nursery when I was 5 years old. I also remember being happy at nursery where I never got off the swing and played happily with the toys. I loved first school which was called Bradford Moor School, but I felt they didn't challenge me enough because I couldn't read until the age of 9 years old. I remember my dad getting angry at the headteacher, then the teachers decided to teach me how to read in year 4. I was special needs but obviously that was not picked up. I think back now, think how unacceptable that was. The good thing in first school was, the students were really nice to me and worked with me nicely. I was so unchallenged that I fell asleep on a bean bag in school. I remember one time; I was only going in school in the afternoon because I was fasting so I was punished by the teacher where she took me by the hand and made me wash some dishes and clean up. The next day I took my mum in and she had an argument with the teacher and got angry and we went home. I was near the school gates, the teacher shouted get back here now. I swore at her from the school gate, I got home and went upstairs where my dad was getting ready to start the day or something. I sat in his pile of clothes and told him what happened. My dad said you have only got one more year to go. The teacher came to my house begging me to come back to the school and she cried, the teacher said "I will lose my job". The teacher said she will not treat me like that again.

I remember a teacher took us to Black Hill; I used to think what an odd person and he gave us Rhubarb to taste, oh it was awful. We used to do ballet as well for P.E where I couldn't get my balance. A lot of children were going to Laisterdyke and I went to Lapage Middle School which was year 5 to 6. I remember finding it quite boring doing my handwriting practice. All the teachers at parent's evening said my writing was untidy. I loved year 6 because we had our favourite teacher. I remember being told to take my scarf off by a teacher so me and my friend went to the headteacher to tell over the racist teacher and the teacher was told off but she was angry and had created an awkward atmosphere. I remember getting an injection and pretending I was in pain because everyone was doing that. A boy use to chase me around the playground and I hated it. I was so happy when he left.

I had two friends called Sobia and Sabrina with whom I went home for dinners with and sometimes got late getting back to school. They had a disco for the older children in school which I didn't agree with, I thought it was over the top. I joined the choir at one point, I only remember singing and making sounds that were foreign to me, sounds like opera singing la la la.

I used to get teased a lot because I wasn't like everyone else but I wasn't afraid to stand up for myself.

I remember hating P.E because I had to get changed in front of the other girls because I felt uncomfortable. I was young, going through puberty and not having a properly fitted bra on. I think you get the picture and I will leave the rest to your imagination. I was so happy when I left middle school.

I started upper school; I went to Belle Vue Girls School in year 9. I remember pushing my dad's car because the car wouldn't start and my friend sitting in the car whilst laughing. I also remember other people who were walking past helping. I found year 9 boring and thinking where am I going to use this in life and I was thinking I don't feel challenged. I was more interested in sociology.

I decided to change schools because of how tough it was to get there. I didn't have the confidence to go to mixed schools because I heard so many bad stories, it put me off. I decided to go to Feversham College, apart from the maths teacher, the rest of the teachers were really good. The maths teacher could never get the attention of the class so she said; 'I am not teaching you' and sat down frustrated. The school was good but didn't have enough resources. I loved listening to the science teacher's family stories. I wanted to learn but I felt like I needed additional support from the beginning of school life, I felt like the education system failed me.

Sarah Kausar

Education in Pakistan 1994, Peshawar

I went to a private school in Pakistan. The school was 20 minutes' drive away, we used to have transportation issues here and there but we never gave up on going to school.

We would start the day with assembly, the whole school would line up, one child would read a surah in a loud voice and we would all listen to it, then it would be the national anthem and then we would read the dua, lab pe atti hai....

We had very gentle teachers and very strict teachers, my favourite teacher was Miss Nasreen, she was my biology teacher.

I loved maths as a child and would do tomorrow's lesson a day before so I knew how to do it in the class on the board. On the other hand, for the subjects I didn't like much I would do their homework in the class in the break before the classes.

I had many friends Ma Sha Allah, I still remember their faces and names.

I used to take parathas for lunch if there was any leftover from breakfast. Also, I would get 2 rupees pocket money to spend in the lunch break with which I would buy a samosa and a crisp packet. On many occasions if I wanted to buy something then I would save up money for it, by skipping buying stuff in the lunch break and would only eat at home around 2pm, (so that was from 7:30 till 2) that was hard but I still managed to do it.

As school uniform, we had maroon coloured kameez and white coloured shalwar and dupattas, black shoes and grey socks. Our nails, shoes and uniforms would be checked daily and if they were not as good as they were supposed to be, we would be made to stand outside our line and then get whacked with a stick on both hands.

If our teacher was absent for whatever reason, and if our class then was a bit loud, we would all be punished for that, whether it was making us stand for the whole class or a whack with a stick, ouch that really hurt. I used to look forward to talking to friends before assembly regarding a cricket match or drama that we watched a night before. I loved every bit of it and miss the old days, like they say old is gold, Meray buchpan ke din kitnay achay thay din.

MA

RB

I belong to the Kaka Kheil caste of Attock. I was born in 1947. I didn't go to school, but learnt to read the Quraan-e-Paak from my Chachi, my paternal uncle's wife. My Chacha, was our local imam.

There were about twenty children from the village who came to learn from my Chachi. She kept a stick to scare us, but never used it. She instilled discipline in us without hitting. The punishment she used was to not move you forward onto the next sabq and nobody wanted to be left behind, so we worked hard. She taught us n'maaz, kalmay and all the religious things we needed to know.

Umm Imaan

I am from Chack Haryaam, in Mirpur. In 1976 I went to Chack Haryaam Primary School. My first memory of schools in Pakistan is standing in lines in the mornings, reading duas, time tables and the national anthem of Pakistan. The older girls would read it out loud and we would repeat after them.

I remember enjoying school, having fun playing with my friends. I went to a mixed school and my older brother used to go with me, so I felt pretty protected. Our school was quite far as it was a couple of villages away. We walked to school every day. In summer we sat outside and in winter indoors. Our school was not a purpose-built school, but someone's house which was used as a school.

We had one teacher initially and then two female teachers. My favourite teacher's name was Fahmeeda. I thought she was kind and made more effort with the children. The other teacher used to bring her baby daughter to school and expect the girls to look after her. I was a fairly bright kid and was favoured by teachers. However, over there kids used to be punished for not knowing their lesson or not doing their homework. The learning was done by memorising from books, stories of prophets, famous people of Pakistan, like Quaid-e-Azam, Alama Iqbal, Aziz Bhatti Shaheed etc. and maths, alongside learning time tables and duas and salah.

Our school uniform was blue kameez and white shalwar and scarf.

When my brother moved to secondary school, I used to walk to school with another girl from my village. We became best friends. I still remember her, though I am not in touch with her anymore. We didn't have lunch in school, we came home and had lunch at home. Sometimes the ice lollies seller came to our school and if we had any money, we bought some from him.

I was eleven when I came to England with fond memories of Pakistan. I had studied till class four. We came to England in September 1980 and started school in April 1981, after the Easter holidays. I went to Usher Street Language Centre. In the eighties all migrants started school life in a language centre. There were all Asians there, it was mixed and I was there for a year and a half.

The first time we sat at desks in twos, the teacher stood in front and wrote on the board. In Pakistan the teachers sat and called the children to them. In England the teacher came to you when you put your hand up. No hitting, no memorising. It seemed pretty easy and chilled.

We were given a book a week to read which was normally a classic from literature. The most difficult part was getting used to the food. Salt and pepper pots used to be left on each table alongside jugs and glasses. At home we still ate the same roti and salan, apart from having more meats rather than the lentils and vegetables we mainly had in Pakistan, which was nicer. At school it was a surprise to taste food that was not salan and it was still flavoursome and nice. I liked meat school dinners. The only thing I didn't like was quiche.

To the English people we were all the same, brown people, but for me it was strange to be in a school with people from different backgrounds. There were people from all over Pakistan, Bangladesh, Afghanistan and India. Our languages and dialects were different, our food was similar, but different. My friends were a Gujrati from India, a Gujrati and a Punjabi from Pakistan. There were also people there that held different religious views from me though we were all Muslim. It was my first time meeting a Shia and those we called Wahabis and much later on I found out that some of the girls were Qadiyanis, but they kept it a secret because they were worried that they will be discriminated against. I don't know how I felt when I found out, they were still my friends, (but I don't know if I still respected them the same, but we still stayed friends with each other.)

When I moved to Carlton Bowling Secondary School, it was a completely different experience. There were about half white children, whilst the other half made up of Asians, Africans and Chinese. It was a big school and we had to move around school to attend our lessons. We had a lot of independence. I really enjoyed my high school. It was really different from all the other schools I had attended so far.

In the eighties, we had a different exam system. It was CSEs, O Levels and A Levels. GCSEs came about in the nineties. I did not go on to further education. I left school at sixteen and started working. At that time my dad was in Pakistan and my mum was struggling financially, so I decided to work. My first job was working in a sewing factory during summer holidays where we got paid per garment we sewed. We started work at 9:00 am in the morning and continued working until 5:pm, with half an hour lunch break. Ladies all sat behind rows of sewing machines and sewed one line of stitching per garment, the next lady doing the next line of sewing.

Then, I got a traineeship with Bradford council through the YTS – Youth Training Scheme, I started working with Bradford Education at Britania house. This was an admin role and I learnt to use a computer.

Food

Liyana Aiza

It was 2018, in Pakistan, in some random market area in a car in the night.

We had barely been there three days and already my mother's younger sister and older sister decided that it was the perfect time to go buy ice cream. The time was after sunset. And it was during November.

My mother just straight up refused. She wasn't insane! She had a then-1 year old!

Unfortunately she was the only sane one. Because everyone else decided to do it.

In true Pakistani fashion we all forced our way into my grandad's ancient creaky cramped car.

There was my older aunt, Rizwana, her baby Kainat, there was my younger aunt Mali and her baby whom for some reason was known as Beezo or Monkey (although considering her mischievous nature I am not surprised), and then me. And we were all in the back.

In the front, my third uncle, Amar, was driving whilst in the passenger seat sat my sister Mubeena and uncle Amar's child (he seemed 5 but apparently was barely 4? I still don't know) Bini. And was my other brother Mo there? I don't recall.

Anyway, we all forced ourselves into a car that didn't have space and we went to go get ice cream, trying our best to ignore my stressed mother swearing that if any of her kids got a sore throat for eating ice cream, we were all gonna get it from her.

So we went, all of us, and bought ice cream. Well, uncle Amar got us these ice creams and we sat in the car and ate them. They were at least a foot high and although looked soft, were hard. It was nothing like I've ever seen. But we ate them in between my aunts either threatening to do something if their babies got sick on account of my uncle (wait was this his plan then?) or wondering what demon possessed him to buy ice creams of that size.

I thoroughly enjoyed it and might have finished an entire one on my own. I might have even helped my sister finish hers.

Then afterwards my family decided that it was the perfect time for soup. Hot soup. Savoury soup. After ice cream.

There was obviously a divide in opinions over this. Who wanted soup right after a cold ice cream?

Well, actually, I did.

I could remember my mother's irate words, and knew that if I got a sore throat, I was done, for agreeing to this hairbrained plan. So, the best way, I decided, to prevent that outcome was to have something hot. Surely it would cancel whatever effect the ice cream would have. And as luck would have it, the agreement was to go get soup.

I wasn't too excited for it. I am known for being picky with my food, and the last time I had Pakistani soup I hadn't liked it very much (admittedly I was something like 7 or 6 at the time and back then I was a notorious picky eater). But as it was to save me from a scolding, I decided to have at least a little. Enough to thaw my throat out at least.

So I took the soup and ate it.

And I loved it.

I absolutely loved it.

I never thought I would. I thought I would hate it. I thought it was strange and kind of gross. I thought it would burn me.

But instead I loved it. I wanted more of it. Even now I still crave it.

And I'm not talking about just the soup.

Sarah Kausar

We ate leftovers with cold chapatti which we warmed up on tawa. When I was younger my mum made many foods, whatever was available such as pendia (ladyfingers) I did try different things but I didn't like spicy foods. I remember my mum made chicken or meat curry with potatoes and peas, sometimes she used potatoes and turnip. I loved it when my mum made spicy egg with tomatoes and onions like a curry. As the years went on my mum experimented with food which went wrong sometimes. I remember my mum making really nice food, when guests were coming. She made rice, roast chicken, saag, samosas and kebabs, I loved eating samosas, eating them with tomato sauce.

My mum made fish and chips every Friday which we adopted from the English people. Even at school, we had fish and chips on Fridays. I remember school dinners which I loved so much. I remember seeing keema rolls, vegetables, small ball potatoes. I wish I could go back to school to have school dinners again and I loved the smell from the canteen. The only thing I didn't like was rhubarb dessert and custard, I remember dreading it.

Nowadays there is too much variety. I remember being healthy because when I started working, my colleague offering me chocolates who got me hooked on it. At first, I was annoyed that she offered me chocolate.

As soon as I started earning money, I started going to Morison's where I was drawn to the cake section where I bought doughnuts, cakes and cream desserts. As more variety became more available such as Halal food, fish and chips not fried in animal fat we ate more. From a young age we were taught to look out for Halal food. Sometimes, without knowing we ate Haram food. We eventually learned what is Halal and Haram.

Ramadan food - 1990s to 2000 MA

When I was young, we used to make pakoras just before iftari so they were hot, sometimes we would still be cooking while the azaan was going on as my dad loved hot pakoras. We would have salad, chatni, Roohafaz, shop bought spicy arwi (kachaloo), freshly cooked naans baked on fired burned tandoor and one curry.

We would eat a shop bought dessert afterwards, made from allobokhara and that used to be sold only in Ramadan, so it was very special and we loved it.

Eid food

On both Eid's, we have a tradition, those who are well off slaughter an animal and then they would do a BBQ, starting with ribs and as soon as they are cooked, we start to eat it straight away while preparing the meat on the skewers. Next, we cooked the liver and then cut it in cubes and wrapped in the fat which is wrapped around the stomach of the animal and it's as thin as paper, and then cooked it for few mins and it's one of the most unique tasting foods. And then we would have the meat cooked on the BBQ just with salt no masalas. Meanwhile the bones would be cooked in a pot, started with melting the fat and then adding the meat and cooking it for 10 to 15 mins, then add onion along with fresh tomatoes and green chillies, finally adding water and cooking it till it was tender. It's one of the tastiest things to eat, so special and so close to my heart as it brings back all the good memories of my childhood.

Winter food

Winter was always welcomed with special foods like kidney bean soup, in which we would put small bite sized naan, pour the soup over it, mix it and eat it with small chopped salad and chutney made from green chillies, coriander, garlic and loads of lime juice.

Another special food was meat kicherri, or plain kicherri with oil and onion tarka. Also, sarso ka saag with scrabbled egg was a delicacy to eat in winter.

Corn on the Cob Season

Whenever corn on the cob season came, my dad would always buy tons, so much that his car would be so full. We would stay up late that night and cook them over an electric heater and because they were fresh green, they would give us electric shocks but that never put us off. We loved eating them.

NS

We lived in a tiny village of five houses and families called Andara in Mirpur. Our little village was on the outskirts of the main village and there were four other houses nearby. Three of the houses had children so we all played together in the surrounding fields, climbing trees, building houses in the sand, jumping down from various size buildings as dares to see who is bravest and playing hide and seek.

I remember one year waking up to find no adults in our house or the neighbours' houses. I was alarmed and scared. The main gate was locked from inside and there was an eerie atmosphere. Later on in the morning I found out that a little baby had passed away soon after birth. According to tradition all adults were at the house where the baby had passed away helping and supporting the family.

All children were being supervised by older siblings in their own homes. No one went out to play, we were all being very sombre and quiet as we could hear the crying of the baby's mum. I remember feeling very, very sad and a little hungry late in the morning and wondering when mum was going to come back. I asked my older sister and she explained that no one is allowed to light fire to cook for three days in the village as it's considered bad manners. I remember it sounding like law written in stone and made me feel more sombre and scared.

As the day wore on, I was very glum and hungry and thought the day would never end when there was a knock on the main gate. My older sister went to open the gate as she was in-charge and none of us little ones dared to open it. When she opened the gate there was a large group of ladies all dressed in white mourning clothes and large chadors stood there, they were all from the next village. They each had a large changere in their hands with a cloth 'taji' covering the contents. They all pulled out delicious looking and smelling rotis. Each lady gave five chapatis to us and went on to knock on the house next door. They had cooked at home and had come to drop off food for all the families in the village.

Each lady gave different kind of chapatti. There was corn flour chapati, spicy matti filled chapatis, sweet ones with makan and sakar chapatis. We hungrily tucked in to the lovely food and sat quietly waiting for our mum to come back home. I don't remember her returning as I must have fallen asleep by the time she returned. I don't have any memories of the next two days either as to if any food was brought over by anyone.

If anyone dies the neighbours do not light fire to cook food out of respect for the family and to show that they are mourning with the family. To this day if anyone dies in the neighbourhood or family, I feel bad if I have to cook.

RB

When I was younger, I liked aloo, ghosht, daal and bindi. I didn't like other vegetables. If a guest came, we would slaughter a chicken from home and make curry with that. Sometimes we made pilau or meat too.

Old traditions

On the first Wednesday of Rajab, lots of huge rotis were made. Then in massive bowls and poozay, like a mat with pure cloth, these rotis were ground into tiny pieces and then butter, sugar-coated fennel seeds, coconut, peanuts, kishmish, gurr and sugar were added. It was all blended and turned into choori. When technology came, people used blenders to mix it all together. The rich families made this and distributed it to the poor in the village. It was also sent to the houses of married daughters. We looked forward to it.

The story behind it was that Bibi Aisha PBUH (peace be upon her) had given this as charity when the Prophet PBUH was ill before he passed away. Then we became more religious and we were told that none of the Prophet's companions continued with this tradition and it is not faraz, an obligation to do so, so it has stopped now. It is considered a bidat now, an invention in religion and frowned upon.
Allah Zaari

If it was too hot and it wouldn't rain, the children would go around the village knocking on doors, and people chased them and threw water on them to invite the rains. They also gave wheat or money to the children. All that was gathered was used to make a daig by Gujjar's, which was then prayed upon and the children ate it. This was so much fun. Sometimes we made a daig of rice and prayed over it and shared it. Sometimes it did rain and we believed it was because of our efforts.

Umm Imaan

We eat a lot of meat as Kashmiris in England. In Pakistan we ate mostly daal and vegetables that were homegrown.

The rotis used to be tandoori in the summer months. We have seven to eight months of summer in our area. My mum would make curry on the tandoor and then make roti on there too. The tandoor would get very hot in that time. Sometimes, other neighbours would come and use our tandoor to make roti in to save on fuel, wood and dried cow dung patties. Sometimes, my mum would take her dough to theirs. If occasionally one of the women was too busy, they would give the dough to their child and ask the neighbour to make the rotis for her. Meats, rice and sweet dishes use to be special occasion food.

One really good tradition around food I remember is when people had a death in the family, they would not cook in their house. They were allowed to grieve in peace for three or four days while extended family members collaborated and took food for them and for their guests. This gave the grieving family the time to just grieve and not have to worry about anything else. In times before mine, people ate from what they brought home that day from a wage and this also relieved them from having to worry about money.

We had land and grew a lot of our own food, so we tended to eat seasonal food. We ate wheat, corn and millet flour rotis and only ate curries made with ingredients that were in season. I don't remember anyone ever having allergies to any food.

We had lunch, breakfast and lighter tea. Our breakfast was always parathas with tea or leftover curry from last night. Lunches were generally tandoori roti with daal or vegetable curry and the dinners was again roti with curry, but the roti would be cooked on the tawa and not the tandoor, so thinner and different texture.

When we came to England our eating habits completely changed. We were all of a sudden eating more meat, less vegetables and even less daal.
That was my mum's cooking. Now with my generation, I think food culture is very different. I cook different types of food, more fusion cooking. I think roti is not the main food anymore. My children are exposed to more international foods, at home and outside. They have more choice now. There are all sorts of international foods available. Back in my days in the early eighties, there was only fish and chips to take away. There were McDonalds and Burger King, but they were not freely accessible.

I feel there is not much of the Bradford I grew up in left. It makes me feel sad.

There is more available to children these days in terms of material things, but at the same time more is taken away from them.

Ramzaan

How to make Lassi (and still not know how to make it)

PUT YOGHURT IN THE BLENDER
Put yoghurt in the blender?
NOT THAT YOGHURT
PUT THAT YOGHURT, AND THEN THE OTHER ONE
Aren't they both yoghurt though?
ONE'S THE SOUR ONE. IT NEEDS TO BE DILUTED BUT
ONLY A LITTLE
Only a little?
I SAID PUT YOGHURT IN THE BLENDER
I did!
PUT MORE IN! WHAT ARE YOU FEEDING, CHICKENS?
You said a little though but here!
STOP NOW, I SAID A LITTLE!
I did put a little but my little isn't enough!
That is not little that is a lot!
WILL YOU STOP COMPLAINING? ADD IN THE SALT!
How much salt?
A LITTLE. OH, STUPID, THAT'S TOO MUCH!
The last time you said little it was a lot!
WILL YOU JUST PUT IN THE WATER? YOU KNOW
WHAT, I'LL DO IT MYSELF!
Why is it my fault for messing up?
Why do I get blamed when I never make it?
YOU SHOULD KNOW HOW TO MAKE IT
YOU DRINK IT EVERY YEAR
HOW CAN YOU NOT KNOW HOW TO MAKE IT?
Because I don't make it
How can I know how to make a drink I never make?
How can I be expected to know what I don't know?

Just because I enjoy the taste doesn't meant I know to make it

It doesn't come to me naturally

JUST STOP YOUT EXCUSES. GO MAKE A SALAD AND SET THE TABLE

I will. I do know how to do that.

Liyana Aiza

Sarah Kausar

For Sehri we would have pratai/toast and eggs, some of my family members had cereal and weren't happy waking up early.

I remember Ramadan used to be short when I was younger but I didn't understand why the times changed every year. I later on found that we follow the moon calendar. My mum prepared fried food such as potato pakoras, samosas and kebabs. My mum also made chicken/ meat curries, homemade pizzas. We made pasta as we got older, we made a spicy version with most recipes. We made it this way so we could enjoy eating these dishes. I cannot eat bland food all the time and I don't like really spicy food, I have to have some spice in it.

My mum added vegetables like turnips and potatoes, peas to our meals. If a meal didn't finish, my mum would mix another meal together which didn't always go down well. My dad use to give us money after we had eaten and we ran to the local shop excited to buy sweets and chocolates.

AB

I am from Attock. I was raised with a lot of love. My grandma wouldn't let us go in the sun or work with animals. My dad grew vegetables and had a shop. He grew: bhindi (okra), shimla mirch (peppers), onions, potatoes, aubergine, watermelons and melon. We also had mango, lemon and orange trees.

During Ramzaan for Sehri we had besan ki roti (gram flour chapati), with onions, a little chillies, salt and coriander, made in the tandoor. We then added makhan on to the hot roti and ate it with lassi and chutney.

For Iftari we had parkoray, which are my favourite and rice with Rooh-afza and shakanji for drinks. Shakanji would give me a sore throat, so my mum forbade me from having it.

I am Hafiz Quran so I led the Tarawee prayers for the women of our village at our house.

RB

During Ramzaan for Sehri time we added boiled buffalo milk to a silver candol (metal pot) and added kiyo and khameeri roti to make choori. This meal ensured you wouldn't feel thirsty during the hot days.

In our area we didn't eat bajra. It was for the chicken. We ate wheat and jawar roti.

For Iftari, we ate jawar, makai and kanak roti with saag and lassi, dehi and makhan.

For the household chores I made tea, aata, cleaned the house, took out water with the bull from the well and took care of the animals. My sister-in-law made the curry and the chapati for all the family. My sister-in-law and I both made the lassi before the electric machines came out.

Ramzaan food traditions in Bradford Moor

At Sehri time my grandkids often wake up and have water and not eat anything. When they do eat, they have paratha, Weetabix or cornflakes.

For Iftari they like pakoras, chawal and curry, eaten as one meal. You can find more things here than in Pakistan as there is more wealth here.

There are four houses in my street who we share food with during Ramzaan and throughout the year. Whenever any of us cooks something nice we send it to the other houses.

When I came to England in 1976, I left my eldest daughter behind. People said the environment there is not suitable for young Muslim Pakistani women. She stayed behind with her Chacha and Chachi. Later on, their son went from here and married her and then called her to England as his wife.

Laitar: This was when it was a busy time on the farm, such as harvest time. The mazdoor, the workmen were paid and fed. At 10am we gave them chai and biscuits or rass. At lunchtime we gave them curry and roti. They had their evening meal at home.

Umm Imaan

Ramzaan has always been seen as a special spiritual time in my house. My mum would always increase her worship and reading of the Quran. We always finish reading the whole Quran during Ramzaan. It was an expectation from our parents. My brothers and my dad always used to go for tarawee prayers. We were lucky the mosque was only a few doors from our house, so my brothers would go by themselves too.

At Sahoor my mum would wake up, make parathas and tea for all of us and then wake us up. My younger siblings were not expected to fast because they were too young, but they always wanted to. I remember once my mum didn't wake them up, so in the morning they decided to fast without eating. They were brought back from school because the headteacher thought they might pass-out or die because it was a June Ramzaan and the fast was for seventeen or eighteen hours. To be able to fast the whole of Ramzaan was such a big achievement, especially if you didn't have to fast. The children used to boast to each other about how many fasts they were able to keep. I still remember my first fast at seven years old. I am sure every child remembers their first fast, it is such a special occasion. I used to tell my children that they are only supposed to keep half a day's fast. They would get double the reward as they ate twice a day. This is a special blessing for children for trying.

Now, I make all the preparations and do the Eid clothes shopping before Ramzaan. I personally don't like shopping while fasting. Every shop, from clothes to food seems to be extra busy during Ramzaan. I only shop for things you can't freeze or store like milk and yoghurt etc.

Throughout Ramzaan especially the children wait for Eid. In the Asian culture children are mostly given money on Eid. They collect all the money and buy whatever they want.

Eid

Eid, 2011

Whodunnit? What happens when too many kids are suspected of one thing

Every Eid, we met with our cousins. Well, second cousins. My dad's cousins really, but they were our ages, so we hung out with the girls, my sister and I, while my brother hung out with uncle and the twins. Either way, it was our thing, we'd go to our cousins or they would come to us. The mums would talk together, us girls together and the twins, great big boys, who were much older than us, were always with my dad. I never spent any time with them.

One Eid, we were minding our business when the twins came into the room and demanded to know, who had been in their room? We all denied it, but they were adamant that someone had gone into their room and made a mess. My little cousin, a year younger than me, told them that 'aunty had to put the baby to sleep there'. The twins rolled their eyes, 'We know, that just messed up the bed. Who messed up everything else?'.

Once again, we all denied it. Two things happened after that; I don't remember the order. I don't remember whether the cricket ball happened before or after, it must have happened after, I think.

The first thing was that they demanded that we squiggle on a piece of paper. When it was my turn I asked, 'can it be any squiggle?' 'Yes, just do a squiggle' they said and with that I did a massive loopy squiggle across the paper, before passing it along. After everyone had done a squiggle, the detective twins announced that they knew who the culprit was, the older cousin.

She got upset and began to deny it. Frustrated that they weren't making any progress, the twins grabbed a cricket ball and declared that if we didn't tell the truth, we'd get hit by a cricket ball. As to be expected of tiny girls when confronted by giant boys, we ran for our lives. I remember running to my mother, but 'uninterested' was an understatement regarding her attitude to our danger.

In the end we were lined up again and finally, my angelic looking younger cousin admitted it all, whilst laughing. No one believed her, so she took us to the twin's room and showed us what she did to make a mess, including grabbing a gift card and squiggling on it, a squiggle that coincidentally matched the squiggle my older cousin had made during the course of the investigation. And that was one of the Eid shenanigans that I remember.

Liyana Aiza

Eid in the 90's Rochester Street

We used to see my mum and dad preparing and cooking together, making the rice masala and meat for the next day so they just needed to add the water and rice.

We used to wake up in the morning, have a bath, put Eid clothes on. We would go downstairs and my uncles would give us money, they were very generous, I would get £20 notes. I would go to the neighbour's house and collect money.

We would all get together, go to the fish and chip shop, buy chips and scallops. We would tell each other how much money we had collected. Our mums would try to take our money from us. We would say no, it's our money. I would keep going to the shop to buy sweets and chocolates.

My cousins would come over and we would greet them and be excited to see them.

In the street, my mum would go to the neighbour's house to say Eid Mubarak.

Sarah Kausar

Umm Imaan

Eid used to be a big occasion in our house. My dad was the eldest brother, so following tradition all his younger siblings and their children would come and spend time with us in our house. My mum also invited her siblings and their families, so she would wake up at 4am to start the cooking. By lunchtime, everything would be ready. The table was too small to fit everyone, so we used to lay a mat and the men and boys use to eat together and then all the women and the girls. If there was enough space, we would all squeeze and eat together. It was so much fun. Probably because mum did most of the work and we did most of the celebrating.

We also used to compare clothes to see who had the nicest clothes. After dinner we got our Eidee. Then we would count it all and see who has got the most.

In the evening, we used to go to my mum's sister's house. She also used to have her in-laws there. The next day we would go to my dad's brother's and all the rest of the auntie's houses. The day after or at the weekend, we would go to my dad's sister's.

Eid used to last for a week. Every house you went to you would see new people from their in-laws' sides. We were generally eating similar food in each house, but it was still so much fun.

I feel Eid-ul-Fitar is anticipated more than Eid-ul-Adha, because of fasting.

For Eid-ul-Fitar we all woke up early, took a bath, wore new clothes and mostly the men would make dua on something sweet and then go and pray Eid prayers and come back and eat. However, on Eid-ul-Adha we woke up, had our baths, wore new clothes and read Eid prayers. Then gave Qurbani and brought the meat back and traditionally had a BBQ and had that as a starter and then cooked the rest of the meat in curry and pilau for lunch. The dua for Eid-ul-Adha was made later compared with Eid-ul-Fitar. Lots of meat was consumed on Eid-ul-Adha. The focus for this Eid was on Qurbani. We divided the meat in thirds: A third we kept at home, one third was for relatives and one third was given in the village and to the poor in Pakistan, but to neighbours here.

These days Eid doesn't seem as much fun. People in England celebrate on different days. The communities from different parts of the world don't unite in celebrating Eid. Some people follow Saudi, some follow the nearest Muslim country, so Eid normally falls on different days. Sometimes, even families are not united, because of the area they live and the mosques they follow.

My parents and siblings and some of my aunties tend to follow Saudi and some of my aunties and dad's side of the family follow Morocco.

I fear sometimes, that in time our kids or grandkids will not celebrate Eid because of the uncertainty and the difficulty in this country with getting time off on different days.

I pray we don't lose these beautiful traditions. I think our strength is in our family culture that we have managed to keep for all these years.

MA

When I was young, we used to get new clothes only on Eid. My mum would buy the fabric from the ladies who used to come to people's houses. That fabric would then be given to a seamstress to be sewn. I used to get new shoes or fancy sandals only on Eids. I would have henna done on my hands using matchsticks and I would be so excited I would wake up in the middle of the night to check if my henna was turning out to be a dark colour or not.

As an adult, I buy clothes whenever I want to, but ten outfits do not give me as much joy as that one outfit that my mum bought and had sewn for me in my childhood.

S

I am from Jhelum in Pakistan. This is what my Eid's were like between 1980 and 1986 during my happy childhood.

Those Eids of childhood spent with parents, siblings and friends were memorable. We stayed up all night, us sisters putting mehnthi on each other and chatting away.

We would rise early and quickly get ready. Mum would begin cooking and the smell of pilau would spread throughout the house. Everyone sat together and ate. Then we would congregate at whichever friend's house had a swing put up for Eid in her courtyard. The adults gave us ten or twenty rupees Eidee and we couldn't have been happier.

We used to wear bangles with joy, spent the entire day playing with friends and the Eid day would pass so quickly. Eid was such a happy day.

My mum would buy the material for our clothes and then sew them herself too. She would then match bangles, sandals and jewellery to our outfits. I loved sparkly studs.

When we were younger mum would fill our entire hands with mehnthi at night and fasten them with a cloth, so they don't spoil the bedding. In the morning when we rose and saw our red hands, we would be so happy. Those happy Eids of our childhood can never be forgotten and nor can they return.

In England I live on my own. The man I left all my loved ones for has left me. These have been awful Eids for me. I don't feel like wearing new clothes or cooking anything. One of my friends invited me to her place on Eid day. I pray Allah blesses her with happiness. I also pray no one is ever separated from their loved ones. Separation destroys a person.

RB

I was born in 1947 and got married age sixteen. When I was young, we had our own shop. For Eid my dad would bring jalebi and mithai to sell and give lots at home, so us kids didn't keep going back to the shop for it. Before we had a shop, we used to have a machine. It ground wheat and jawar and chopped their stalks. In our shop we sold sweets, patasay, daal, khal, gur and everything of daily need. I served if my dad was out.

On Eid we received two rupees each. We were bought one suit on Eid and we saved it for big Eid too. The clothes were bought from sellers at home and shops. Our shops were in Campbellpur, Hazro where the main bazaar was.

We wore whatever mum bought for us. The clothes would be sewn by a tailor in the village. Sandals and shoes were new too. I didn't like bangles; I've never worn them. My children do. I wore mehndi, plain on full hand and lines across each knuckle.

We had four huge beir trees in our courtyard. We often had a swing and everyone from the village came and used it. We sometimes got tired too of the people and the mess.

We are farmers. I remember the wheat harvest, the corn and drying it on the roof and gathering people to beat it and using the grains to eat and the rest for fuel. We used jawar to eat and the stalks to burn. We grew cotton too, harvested it, weaved it then sold it. Kept the waste and fed it to the buffalos. We grinded seed and made oil from them.

On Eid day we ate pilau, zarda, kheer, chicken from home, wheat and makai roti, lassi, makhan, yoghurt and ghee.

Migration

Taste

I am from Bradford Moor. The first time I visited Pakistan, I was a little girl. I think I was ten years old. We were there for a month and for that month, our time was spent at my mother's childhood home, a large house, but an old one. That and visiting relatives and the frustrating clothes shopping as I was in-between sizes and I couldn't fit into women's clothes or the children's sizes. That month passed quickly; I had a sip of Pakistan.

The next time I went as a teenager, turning 15 whilst I was there. We were there for three months. This time I had an overflowing drink of Pakistan. Whether it was that I was older or it was that I was there for longer, but I did truly taste that life. Washing the clothes by hand, sweeping the entire yard and washing it at dawn every day, I was able to see it all. I was able to see what life was like for them, the good, the bad and the chaotic. The chaos of that life took over me.

The taste was overwhelming, but it wasn't flavoured much. What I know of Pakistan is what I have seen through the life of my mother's family. The stories of one family.

I haven't fully tasted Pakistan yet. The UK is where I am now. It's calmer, it's familiar. It's orderly. I like the taste here. Its familiar and I prefer it.

But occasionally, I get a hint of that other taste. The taste of chaotic family nights with everyone talking about anything, of nights in a cramped car driving to buy street food, of days in the market of eating the corn on the cob that my aunt insisted she bought for us.

Sometimes, I wonder what it would be like to have a full meal.

Liyana Aiza

Sarah Kausar

When I was younger, about 7 years old, my life in England was playing in the street, going to Attock Park which wasn't called anything at the time. There were a lot more English people around, Sikh and Hindu's and people who were Pashtoon. My best friends were Pushto. I had a friend who I hung out with regularly and with her brother as well. At the time, Attock Park was a huge hill with a white square stone on the top which we sat on. One side had grass on and the other side had stones on it. We used red bread crates to slide on the hill and when we finished, we used to take them back to where we got them from. We played with marbles, pebbles, pitu was a game where you put different size stones on it and threw a stone at them. We used to have crate races where our mums use to be outside chatting and watching us.

Some ladies had a tandoor in their gardens and they all gathered in each other's garden making roti together and having a laugh. The tandoor was made of a chimney which was cemented with a steel bin and there was a wood table next to the tandoor. We burned wood wherever you could find it from, to make the tandoor hot. When it was hot enough, my mum started make shupatte that were thick. My mum use to make us shupattes and put a stick through it. We would hold it like a lolly pop and eat it.

My mum and her friend booked a cheap flight to Pakistan, Karachi. We went on a train somewhere in Pakistan to someone's house where I remember having breakfast. The train was dark and had a hole we had to step over to go into the other carriage. My sister was sleeping on the top bunk. We had to sit squashed together because the train was packed. We were picked up by my friend's relative, the truck was loaded with our suitcases. Everyone got in the truck and there was no more room so they put my mum's friend's son on the edge of the truck and me on the other end. I don't know about him but I was so scared that I might fall off and I held on very tightly. I remember the streets were clean and the houses were so beautiful with verandas.

There was an earthquake and the wardrobe started shaking and my mum said get up and come outside. We stood all together as a family and we prayed; my mum was crying. I thought we were going to die because my mum panicked as usual and told us the walls could fall on us. I started to cry as well. In the morning we went to my cousin's house and he was showing off that he wasn't scared.

I used to go to the shop and buy paaper (crisps) and sweets for one rupee. I loved the orange circle sweets. I went by myself to my mum's family's house and my dad's sister's house and on the way, I would stop by and talk to them. Also, I would go to my great grandma's house where there was a girl but at the time, I didn't know who they were and how they were related to me. Later on, I found out they were my grandma's brother's children. I remember meeting a girl who lost her mother, she showed me her before she was going to get buried and told me she had to look after her siblings. In the street lived a girl named Nazia who was a lovely, kind girl, and I remember her sister coming to our house taking water from our well which had to be pulled up with a bucket tied with a rope and then you turn the handle. There was another friend who bragged about her dad having a lot of money. She had a lot of cool toys and things.

I eventually missed home and asked my mum when we were going back to England.

Our first day in England

We arrived in September 1980. We came to London and my dad collected us from the airport. When we came, snow had already fallen and we arrived in Bradford over four hours later.

The house was much smaller than our house in Pakistan. It was nice and warm. There were a lot of white people and Sikhs in this area then. There was a good number of Muslim families too. Both of our neighbours were Sikhs. My mum could not understand them properly. Their accents were really strong and they spoke proper Punjabi. There was a good mixture of nationalities living together. It felt really safe.

We lived at the end of the street. There were no through roads. It was the widest part of the street and we played in front of our house. My friends from school lived in the same area and we played hopscotch, pitoo and marbles in the street. We felt safe all the time. It was clean.

Two of my aunties lived a few streets away from us and we were always running back and forth from their houses.

I was eleven at the time. Now, I would not allow my eleven-year-old to walk these streets alone. We used to have so many facilities in this area: a decent library and youth clubs. They used to hold lots of events during holidays and invite storytellers to come to the library. There were children's areas where you could sit and play and read with your child. Now, when I go to the same library it makes me sad to see that there is not much left of it. The big Central Library is also closed. It was one of the best assets of Bradford. The city centre was big and bustling. We used to have big brand names like House of Fraser, Rackham's, Sunwin House, British Home Stores etc. We had lots of specialist shops too.

When I started working in the mid-eighties, I loved browsing in these shops. It was such a happy place to be. There were quite a few bakeries, sandwich shops and hot food takeaways in the city centre. Now there is hardly anything left.

The community atmosphere is gone. Even though we were financially less off, there was a different kind of unity and togetherness. I don't feel that anymore. It feels like a different area now.

Umm Imaan

MA

I came to Bradford from Peshawar in 2003. I was twenty-one years old and eight months pregnant and told the flight attendant I was seven months as I was huge and afraid, she might not allow me to travel.

In Peshawar we had a huge haveli with mulberry and chinar trees in the courtyard. We had a dog, chickens and goats. My cousin was married in Attock. A lot of men from there worked in Hong Kong and came to the UK from there. I married in her family and ended up here in Bradford.

RB

I came to England in 1976. I brought three children with me from Pakistan and had three children here. My children are well educated, my daughter teaches in Dewsbury, my son spent seven years to complete his Hifz in Nottingham and now teaches in a local masjid, my other son studied at a boarding school in Bury and now teaches at the local masjid.

TA

I was my mother's spoilt child and the hardships I faced were of equal weight. I had a happy home life, children and a loving husband who is a doctor. As my son got older, I noticed he didn't really engage with learning. I didn't understand why, so I spoke to his teachers and they said he just likes playing, so we don't bother to try and teach him and just let him play. I thought well they know best.

Then my sister came to visit us who was a teacher in London. She said to me, don't mind me saying this, but your son is special, take care of him. Now that I understood, I moved him to a special school. He stayed in a hostel. On the weekends the rest of the children went to church and we hired a Qari for our son. He learnt Surah Kahf and enjoyed that.

When he was sixteen, we felt that the school didn't meet his potential, so we researched and found that there was a school in Pakistan that gave skills-based training to young people with special needs, and so in 1984 we moved to Pakistan. We put him into a private special school there and he really enjoyed it.

Unfortunately, during a pottery session one of the teacher's had put pressure on him to do better and he refused to go back to school. We let him take a few days off, but he then point blank refused and said he does not like that teacher and won't go back. Our extended family encouraged us to get him married as he was our only son and that our line will continue. Some poor family would give their daughter to us as we were well off. However, we did not want to put a girl through this.

In his thirties, we were looking after our son and one day as my husband tried to help him up, he fell on top of my husband and my husband was hurt. He then developed bedsores. One day a relative visited and said to me, 'Pray that God takes your son before he takes you.' It made me very angry. Later on, I reflected and thought my son is suffering and I prayed to Allah that he is one of his special people, who does not deserve to suffer and to please take him. He passed away soon after that. Our daughter is married, but cannot have children. I am grateful for my life and like to come to the sessions at Attock Park and show women to do crochet and knitting and enjoy the chit chat, but be close enough to go and check on my husband, who is now elderly and ill.

Our daughter lives in Pakistan and we will visit her soon.

Discrimination

Woman's Life

Wear your clothes neatly

Don't make yourself a disgrace

Keep your voice down

Do you want them to stare at your face

You are a treasure

As precious as gold
Get married as soon as you can
Before you know it you'll be old

The boys can laugh
we let them play
The daughters need to work
They'll be mothers one day

The man makes a mess
But it's alright
He's been working all day
Let him rest at night

The woman is angry
But she must hold her tongue
Do not nag the husband
For his day has been long

A woman's job is easy
Simply stay at home
Cook, clean, raise the kids
Never mind you do it on your own

It's fine if he's angry
He's worked all day for you
You, woman, stay quiet
Do what you're supposed to do

When she shouts subdue her
Remind her of her place
If she lets her house stay messy
Then she's known as a disgrace
No matter what he does
You must stay together
Endure it you must
Or you'll be alone forever

Keep the father of your kids there
Never mind his anger then
You remove yourself from him
You'll never be married again

No matter how old he is
He'll always find a wife
You, you have a time limit
Such is a woman's life!

Liyana Aiza

Sarah Kausar

When I was little, Bradford Moor was a very mix area. In our street there were English people, Pakistani and Indians. It was a clean area. One lady used to knock on the door of ten houses and invite all the ladies out to help and clean the street saying it was our kids that played here. All the women came out happily and they all cleaned the street.

One night I remember this Hindu guy was drunk and he was weeing in the street. In the morning I saw the women out washing the path and the road. We took pride in our area. It has gone downhill now. People don't come out anymore. My sister jokes that women have barricaded themselves inside their homes.

Sadly, in our area even then we didn't all play together as children. Muslim, Hindu and white parents told their children to play with their own and to stay away from the others. I think they were scared us children would convert to each other's religions.

The white people could be quite racist and often called us Pakis. There was this one elderly white lady who had a garden full of flowers, she talked to us. If they were nice, we talked to them too.

In Pakistan we had some neighbours who were really rich. I got on with their daughter and she let me play with her toys, but my parents told me I couldn't play with her again. I don't know why, but I still remember they had a blue door and she was really nice.

One day I came back from school and asked my mum what Moachi (cobblers/shoemakers) meant? Our parents never told us anything, so we were quite naïve about castes and things like that. I wish they had told us stuff and explained it. My mum just said, 'We are Hinko and Muslim, that's all you need to know'. There are stereotypes about all communities. Pathan are seen as 'daaday', feisty and strict. My cousin lives in Birmingham and she said to me, 'We are Chachi and they fear us here.'

Umm Imaan

My dad came to England in the early 60s. He worked in the mills until the mills closed down in the eighties. I remember him telling us that where two white men were given a machine to manage, one Asian man was given one on his own. In essence doing the work of two men and getting paid for one. I do remember my dad saying that they were paid less than their English counterparts.

At school I don't remember facing that much discrimination. Our school was a good mix of Asians and English people with the Africans and Chinese in the minority. We didn't really have many teachers from minority groups. Only the Asian language teachers who were not English.

I started working in the mid-eighties for Bradford Council. There were at times, comments made, which looking back now were not appropriate, but generally I don't remember facing much discrimination. I think my generation was the first to go into white collar jobs. I remember my aunt's husband with a law degree from Cardiff University working as a bus conductor. He was never able to do the Legal Practise Course; him or his brother.

I remember one of my English colleagues repeatedly asking me why Asian magazines continuously use European models in their every edition and not as many Asian models. At one point I had enough of it and replied that because European women take more off for less and the Asian models will only model certain types of clothing. I don't remember him asking me that question again. Generally, I remember good experiences during the 80s and 90s.

I noticed a clear change in people's behaviour towards me after 9/11 and that continues until today. My eldest daughter went to a private school for sixth form and the amount of discrimination she faced not only from fellow students, but also from teachers was unbelievable. I didn't send the others there even though they offered scholarships. It wasn't worth putting them through that even for free.

I remember during secondary school one of my daughters expressed an interest in becoming a pilot to her career's adviser, who scoffed at her and told her to try social work. I do think Asian and Black kids have to do twice as well as white kids to be given the same opportunities. My eldest told me her teacher was visibly disappointed when she got an A* in English Language at AS Level, while the white kids got grade C's or less.

My children had similar experiences at university. Apparently, lecturers' mentality towards Asian medical students is that they are forced by their parents to be there and not there by choice. That sort of views was abundantly found amongst the consultants too during their training. My daughters are all doctors and they have all experienced similar attitudes. The assumption is made that they want to specialise in general practise and most Asian girls then opt for becoming a GP. Not to belittle GPs, but to point out the mentality and expectations that are held towards our children. My daughters say when they decide they want to become consultants their superiors' faces just drop.

I feel my children face more discrimination than what I did. I feel it is getting worse rather than better. The insecurities and fears I feel living here now, I didn't feel them in the 80s.

Funerals

It's hard to mourn what you don't have. It's a funny thing about death in the family. Particularly when you're the third culture kid who has had little to no real contact with her family growing up.

When my mother's grandmother died, I didn't even know she had a grandmother. I was perhaps 6, maybe 7. It was Eid day, and what I noticed was that my mother was yelling into the phone during the mandatory once a year Eid phone call to Pakistan. I knew she was upset and I tried to ask what happened but she shut me down. Later I learnt her grandmother had passed away. Much later I learnt that her grandmother had passed away months ago but they kept it a secret only for my grandma to accidentally let it slip on Eid.

I didn't feel anything.

When I was 10, my little cousin died. She was killed by an electric shock. I found that out when we went to Pakistan and they told my mother. I woke from my nap and came out to see my mother in tears, and then I was told that she had in fact died a while ago and told my mother now after she showed the doll she took for her.

I didn't really feel anything.

When I was 13 my dad's grandmother and aunt died. I had actually met them both once.

But yet again, I didn't feel anything.

Often I hear my mother on the phone. A name is mentioned, a gasp of shock, and everyone is talking about death. And again, I don't feel a thing.

Because to me, they're just names. Just like to them, I'm just a name. It's hard to mourn what you don't have.

Liyana Aiza

Sarah Kausar

When I was younger, I remember my long-distance cousin's dad passed away. At the time, the funeral was done in the back garden. I have a strange memory like he was in a cot style bed. There were so many people in the garden crying.

When my mum's mum passed away, we had no home phone so a lady in the street broke the news to my mum. They sat on a stool and started crying together trying to comfort my mum.

When my long-distance cousin passed away, he was under 25 years old. It was a sudden death because he stopped breathing one night, I think he had asthma. I remember the back street was a road and they were crying so much and dressed in white.

When my dad passed away, it was a big shock, we were crying a lot. My mum broke the news to me, I was absolutely devastated. My dad passed away in Pakistan while on a motorbike and a car hit him, knocked him off the motorbike. My cousin was with him because my dad didn't know where the land was so he could put walls around it, so no one would try to steal the land. I remember people saying death was calling him and it was his time to die. I found it comforting that it's meant to be.

My dad died straight away with internal bleeding. My cousin was rushed to hospital. Someone recognised my dad and my cousin, they called my cousin's brother.

Before my mum left for the airport, I hugged my mum, she said be strong and she was very emotional. Ten tickets were booked for Pakistan and a lot of the family flew out. As they were leaving, I wanted to go away with them but I was 8 months pregnant. My daughter is 11 years old now. Each year that goes by, my daughter ages and I never forget how many years it has been. My cousin was with me, it was nice to have her with me, so many people came, I didn't recognise them. Different ladies from the street, sent food from their houses, it was mainly meat dishes.

My mum in Pakistan got food made and gave it to Madrassas. They did it every Thursday until 40 days. I don't really understand why they do this ritual.

Funerals are now held in Masjids; people use the seeds of dates to read first
Kalimah. People hug the loved ones of the deceased person. Sometimes ladies send food to the Masjids and catering is used as well.

I remember my grandma passed away, we all gathered around her and cried and hugged each other. I was showing her daughter on video call, her mum's body and holding my mouth shut and we closed her eyes. I remember my auntie saying, she died smiling. The men came to collect the body to take it to the Funeral home. I remember the ladies saying we need to go the Masjid. We took tea pots and other dishes to the Masjid. My grandma was cleaned and put in the coffin with white cloth to cover her. My mum let the men of the family say their goodbyes. Then the women were allowed to say their goodbyes.

Umm Imaan

The rituals for funerals are the same for men, women and children. As soon as someone passes away, all of the extended family is notified so they can take part in the funeral prayers.

Meanwhile, before rigor mortis sets in, a piece of cloth is used to support the mouth from dropping by rapping it from under the chin and tying it gently on the head, all other limbs are straightened and the face is turned towards the right. Sometimes, a slight pressure is applied to the stomach to release any wind etc. The first clean-up is done immediately.

Then people come and pay their respects. Once the doctors have seen the person and the death certificate is issued, the body is taken for ghusal. The ghusal is normally given by close family: daughters and sisters for women and sons and brothers for men. We believe that the deceased has a right on the family to prepare them well for their next journey. As far as I am aware, there are only three pieces of white material for males and five pieces for the female to be wrapped in as a shroud. The materials must not be sewn. The women have an extra sheet to cover her with and also a scar to cover head.

For women, normally only females are allowed to see her face and men who are considered mahrams, e.g., sons, brothers, nephews and husbands etc.

The ritual of the ghusal is mainly done in the way that a living person would make wudu and take a bath. The body is never exposed fully even to people who wash it. For people stand holding a long piece of black or white material over the body with enough gap for the person who is doing the washing to be able to put their hands in and comfortably wash. Then the body is wrapped up, ready for the funeral prayers (janaza).

The imam of the mosque normally performs the prayers. In England the prayer is mostly performed in the mosque. In Pakistan it is performed in an open ground, so as many people can take part. They say if more than forty people take part in the janaza and pray for the forgiveness In Shaa Allah the prayer is accepted. The more people the better.

After that, the body is carried to the graveyard where the grave is normally already dug and ready. Then the mahram men normally lower the women's body into the grave. In men's case it is preferred that his next of kin do the last rituals, but others can also do it or take part in it.

It is believed that after the burial process is completed, the family members should stay by the graveside and make dua for as long as reasonably possible. As Muslim we believe the ruh, the soul, is still attached to the dunia, the world, and feels sad if we leave straight away as it hears the footsteps fading away. Also, the questioning of the body only begins when the last person has left.

Officially, the public mourning period should only last three days. However, a wife is allowed to mourn her husband for four months and ten days. It is called iddah. During this time, she should be taken care of by the family. Her and her children must be provided for. She must be given this time to grieve in peace must not be given responsibilities. After this period has passed then she can decide to remarry or not, it's her choice. This gives the woman time to come to terms with her loss and decide for her future. I have experienced all of this, but found it easier to say it as though talking about rules.

I am from Gujar Khan and I was there when my grandma passed away in 2000. If a death happens in our home the first thing, we do is check the person who has died. Close their eyes and their mouth, face them towards the Kaaba. We straighten their legs and fasten both of the big toes together to keep the legs straight.

Then we tidy up the house, so it is ready for guests. Then we do the preparations for the ghusal. After this first ghusal we wrap them in a clean cloth so that afterwards whoever gives the second ghusal doesn't have the trouble of having to remove their clothes.

We then arrange for the food to be served and set a time for the janaza prayers. After the janaza, the men go to the graveyard and we invite the women to come and eat. Whilst the body is in the house, we sit around pray, read the Quran and pray for the soul's forgiveness.

The first day's food comes from the women's family in our tradition. This leaves the immediate family free to grieve. In my family the first day's food came from Hala's, my mum's sister's and the second day's breakfast came from my Mamu's, my mum's brother's house.

After the burial we plant a flower bush on the grave and after the janaza prayers we use to distribute fruit amongst the men.

On the third day we arrange the Qull, prayers and a feast. Then for the next forty days we said prayers over food after Asar each day. People offered the fortieth prayers and feast after forty days, but some people if they needed to could offer them after ten or thirty-five days too. In our family's people brought us white shawls or suits after forty days. We then hold a prayer and feast event on the anniversary.

RB

For three days no one cooked at home. Men sat at the hujra. Women sat together at home. In olden days the neighbours brought the food around. Now daigs are bought from the bazaar for the family and the guests. Kulal in Pashto is the chef who made the food.

Weddings

Strict Pattan Weddings

They're meant to be fun occasions. Music and food. Dancing. All good stuff.

Of course, I hadn't been to many. Why? Because most people are invited to weddings of friends or family. I had no family here in Bradford, and my few friends were a bit young to be getting married. However, my introverted dad did have the odd friend who had someone in the family getting married and that's how we ended up going to a wedding of someone we never knew existed.

"Separate places for men and women, right?" my mother wanted to confirm. Covering her face meant that men being around was going to make eating slightly difficult.

"Oh, yes. It's a strict pattan wedding," my dad said with full confidence. That was good, it meant it wasn't going to be like the last wedding I'd been to where the men kept coming into the women's hall.

Well, we got there and settled down at our table. All well and good until the men showed up.

Because of course how could a strict pattan wedding be complete without all the men coming up with the bride and invading our privacy?

I lost count of how many men and who they were pretty quickly. One was a groom, the rest were God knows who. And they were everywhere.

I could live with that. I could not live with the camera man.

I have nothing against wanting to take pictures. I do however not understand why it was so necessary for him to take pictures of the people eating.

Why? What was so interesting about people chewing rice? At least it provided me with some basic amusement as I watched my mother play the game of trying to sneak bites of rice under her niqab when the camera wasn't pointed in our direction - which I remember to be weirdly always on us.

As soon as we went into the car, the first thing my mother did was to quote my dad's words back at him. "Strict Pattan Wedding, huh?"

My dad just laughed. "Whoops."

At least I got some free entertainment out of it. And we didn't have dishes to wash at home either.

Liyana Aiza

Sarah Kausar

My earliest memory is going to a mehndi where I had samosas and pakoras. I remember my mum encouraging me to go to events like this. The lady who invited us to the wedding, taking loads of people up the street and banging a drum. I remember going to weddings at Karmand Centre. The ladies danced at the end when most of the guests left. I went to a cousin's wedding, where the women were in a tent.

The mehndi took place in the back garden, when we were younger like under 10. The mehndi usually took place in people's home where they would show you the clothes of the bride. The clothes would be hung up on something like a washing line, some of the accessories would be laid nicely on the bed, gold and handbags. People saw traditions in other weddings and would copy and do those activities in their own weddings. My cousins wedding, it was an excuse to have a party such as having a pyjama party or haldi party. Nowadays people have chocolate fountains and sweets for the kids and people like adding favours like little boxes of sweets.

The last wedding I went to, the couple walked down the path to the stage and they took pictures and cut cake and also there was a DJ.

My cousin's wedding was quite modern and it was in a hotel. Her husband's friends said some nice words and she wore a white dress. It seemed like an English wedding with Asian food. My kids, nephews and the neighbours' children walked down the aisle with a sign. Some weddings I went to, the couple were very shy walking down the aisle.

In most Asian weddings, you are invited to come and eat a meal. The host welcomes the guests at the entrance and goes around the hall to make sure everyone has eaten.

RB & AFB

I came to England in 1976 with three young children.
AFB: I came to England in 1978 with two children, a three-year-old and a one-year-old.

This is the order of our wedding rituals in Attock:

1. Deh rakhte hein. You set the date for the wedding. People are fed chawal and roti etc.

When the boy's family came for the furniture and jahaiz, the girl's family put colour and water on them as a laugh.

2. Galiyaan – lots of days of singing wedding songs.

3. Mahiyun and mehndi together - Mehndi: the girl's side offered kahaar, boiled eggs and milk to the maraaj and his friends. Then the groom and his friends gave money. The girls' brothers fed the groom.

The girl's family teased and locked the door and took money for opening it.

4. Then doli, the bride's carriage' went the second day. The girl's family only fed a meal to their own guests. The boy's baraat were fed tea, namak paare and mithai. The boy's side fed their own family when they got home.

Third day (triyaa) at in laws: Ladies from the village gathered, ate snacks. The girl kept trying on all the clothes she was given. Approximately a dozen outfits. And matching handbags, shoes and jewellery.

On the 5th or the 7th day the girl's family invited the boy's family for a meal. Sometimes she stayed a night and then went. The sisters-in-law hid the grooms' shoes and demanded money.

Clothes given as gifts: a few days or weeks before the wedding, clothes are given to all close relatives, men and women. Some people get those sewn and wear them.

Makeup: In our days the makeup was face powder, lipstick, surma (kajal) and sakra (walnut bark to give colour to the gums).

Hair wax: we braided our hair with thin plaits and then put a perfumed water over the braids.

Mehndi: full hands and feet

Food on weddings:

Mehndi day: salan, roti, halva, chaval

Walimah: sometimes buffalo, sometimes cow or bull meat, chawal (rice), and halva (semolina pudding).

Doli carried to the house on shoulders of close family members of the groom.

As the daughter left the parents' home the girl was given dry rice and she threw the rice forwards and backwards.

The weddings here in England are the same.

Differences:

Some people do tiyaa, others don't.

Girls don't always wait for 5 or 7 days after the wedding, sometimes they come to their parents sooner.

AB

My nikah took place in 2004 in Attock. My wedding happened in Bradford Moor in 2008.

Mehndi: This took place at home here. Neighbour's daughter put mehndi on me. The design was not nice and colour was okay. My in-laws bought me mustard colour clothes and I got dressed. It was just a women's event and my husband did not wear mehndi.

The baraat day was home too. All my in-laws came. They took me from my sister-in-law's house to my in-laws nearby.

Walima: This was in a hall, at the Venue. It was a segregated event. It was a lovely day. I wore a red and white lehnga, with matching jewellery and makeup.

Differences in weddings Pakistan and here:
When men in Pakistan go to a girl's house, fulfil all the rituals, then they feel the responsibility of bringing someone's daughter home. Over here, the way my wedding happened, they don't feel the weight of it and don't care.

And if they do, the families don't like it and interfere, ensuring no happiness can ensue.

Umm Imaan

I am from Mirpur. Where we came from, we mainly married into our own caste only. Very rarely if there weren't enough girls the men would marry women from other castes, but a girl was never allowed to marry out of caste. So, generally you would have known your husband and his family your whole life.

The first event after the families have agreed to marry their children to each other would be for the boy's family to go to the girl's family with other women from the village to formally announce that they have chosen this girl and set a date for the wedding. In return the girl's family would give dry fruits and other gifts in a big bundle to take back and put yellow colour on the bundle (usually wrapped in a white cloth to be carried back on the head) and on the women's clothes who came.

In the following days the boy's mother would invite family and friends and open the bundle, all sing together and show everyone what they were given and distribute the food contents between everyone. This would be the official start of the wedding.

In the girl's house from then on, the girl would be treated like a guest in her parent's house. She would not be allowed to do any housework.

Her parents would choose the dowery etc. She would however be allowed to choose her own clothes. In well off families, she would get up to thirty to forty outfits with shoes, jewellery, handbags etc. plus gifts in gold from both sides.

Traditionally, the girl's parents would give smaller gold sets and the boy's parents were expected to give the bigger pieces of jewellery, such as necklaces, choomar and bangles.

There would be dholki events every night at the boy's side all the way up to the actual big day. Family and friends would get together, play instruments and sing wedding songs.

In the week leading up the wedding, they would have an event called maniyaan. First the boy's side and then the girl's side. The boy's and the girl's families, friends and extended family would be invited to each other's houses and have a big feast. This is the beginning of many celebrations to come.

The next celebration is mehndi. Again, the boy's family do it first and then the girl's family and the family are invited and a feast is had. This is mainly a women's event, but men from close family (uncles, cousins, brothers etc.) are present as well. Mainly to manage the event.

For this event, the girl is dressed up and sat on the stage and the women come and put some henna on her hand and some oil in her hair, by dipping a finger in a pot of oil and wiping it on her head. Normally a leaf is placed on her hand and henna is placed on the leaf. This is to keep her hand clean so later the mehndi artist can make designs on her hands and feet. This is normally done two or three days before the wedding.

The last day is normally left for rest for the bride and groom and for the family to make the preparations for the main days.

All the events are managed by the close family. These days waiters are hired or the venue provide a full service. Everything is managed by them.

Normally, the first day, baraat, is paid for by the girl's family. They welcome all the guests with the groom. It is called baraat or janj. The groom and his family are stopped before they enter the house or venue and the groom and his friends are given a welcome drink, which is normally milk and some sweets, mithai. The milk is offered by the bride's sisters, cousins and friends and they then demand money for it. This is seen as one of fun parts of the wedding and everyone takes part in it wholeheartedly, with the boy's side teasing with pennies and the girl's side demanding more and more. The mithai is distributed between all the guests.

Then everyone is invited to enter. The nikah is read and a huge feast is had. At the end of the day the groom's family ask the girl's parents permission to leave and take the bride home. The groom especially goes to his new mother-in-law to thank her for giving her daughter to him.

When the girl is leaving her parent's house, the Quran is held over her head by her older brother, which symbolises that she is leaving her family home in God's protection. Also rice or wheat is held in front of her again by brothers in a tray and the bride will take hands full and flick it over her head where there would be people mainly family with a cloth to catch the grains. The seeds are fed to birds as a form of charity.

When they get to the groom's house, the bride normally refuses to enter their house as part of the fun traditions and demands money. The groom's parents then give her money as a gift before she enters the house.

Then the bride is served something sweet, generally chooree (ground chapatti, blended in pure butter and sugar), which is supposed to be made by the groom's mum to start their new life on a sweet note.

The second big day of the wedding is Waleema, which is paid by the groom's parents, mostly inviting their own family, friends and the bride's close family. At the end of this day the bride is taken back to her parents' house from the grooms.

Then after a day or two, the groom and his family again come and they share a meal with the bride and her family in a small private ceremony. The bride leaves for the final time as part of the wedding traditions and goes to her forever home. This marks the end of the official celebration and festivities. After this, the bride and groom are free to come and go and do things at their own will.

Jinn Stories

Umm Imaan

As a Muslim I believe jinn exist. They were sent on earth before humans and that there are more of them than humans. They are made of smokeless fire. There are many jinn stories, how true they are I don't know. These are the few that my mum told me about.

My mum said that when she was a young kid, her dad had a friend who a jinn had befriended. Once he came to their house to see granddad and the children starting asking him about this jinn friend. They wanted to see proof and know if it was the truth. So, he told them to put a bowl inside their house and come and join him in the garden. My mum told us that they did that. After a while he told them to go and pick it up. She said that when we got the bowl, it was full of apples and that apples were not even in season in our area.

Another story she told us about the same person is that one day him and granddad were walking home late from visiting other friends and all of a sudden, he curled up in a human ball and rolled down a cliff. When he reappeared, he had some sweets in his hand which he offered to granddad and told him they were from his shop. Obviously, granddad didn't feel comfortable or want the sweets and just wanted to go home.

Once he told them that the jinn gave him a bucket full of gold and told him that if he tells anyone where he got it from the jinn will take it all back. Otherwise, he can sell the gold and live a good life. In the morning he took some gold to his older brother and told him to sell it and then he didn't have to work anymore. They were tailors by trade. Not surprisingly his brother got very suspicious and demanded to know where he got it from. At first, he didn't tell. Then his brother threatened to kick him out of the house because he didn't want any trouble with the police in the family home, thinking he probably stole if from somewhere. At the end with a lot of family pressure he gave in and told them how he got the gold. Apparently when they went in the house to have a look, the bucket was not there. It had disappeared.

When I was about seven or eight years old and we lived in Pakistan, one evening before bedtime we went out to relieve ourselves before going to bed. In the distance I saw a ball of fire walking, heading in the opposite direction. I believe that was a jinn I saw.

Another story I heard was when I lived in the Midlands. One of my friends rang and told me that there is a jinn in her house, because her cooker keeps turning on by itself. Sometimes they turn the gas on and don't light it. Apparently, she had a shed in the garden and on the day, they decided to get rid of it because they didn't use it much.

When they got rid of it, these things started. She believed the jinn lived in the shed and it upset them that they got rid of it. After reading Surah Baqarah and Azaan in the house frequently, she managed to get the jinn to leave the house. After about a week of doing all this, the jinn left. My friend was told by the rakki she called that they didn't want to hurt them, just to scare them and cause mischief as they were upset with them. Now, they will not bother them again.

Other stories I have heard are where people say that their lights are turned on by themselves. One woman used to say that as soon as they go upstairs in the evening, the lights downstairs come back on and sometimes she heard movement in her house.

Generally, I have been told that the jinn don't like being near humans. They travel after sunset and rest during the day after sunrise. Their living pattern is opposite to ours. May God protect us from these kinds of encounters.

Humour

Umm Imaan

I remember my parents telling us of a lady who lived in the area. She went to the local shop to get some eggs, but couldn't speak any English. She looked at the shopkeeper, made cockerel noises and placed her hand at her bottom. The shopkeeper nodded and gave her a tray of eggs!

Poems

A story told in rhyme

A young man got married and his family said to him, 'women are very cunning, so be careful'. The young man went to work abroad and kept sending money to his wife. When he came back, he asked his wife, 'I sent you exactly this amount of money, tell me where have you spent it?'

The woman replied with a poem. The poem is in Pahari/Pothwari and it rhymes which adds to the enjoyment, but here is a translation:

The total you sent was 100 rupees
Your father died; I spent 20 rupees on that
That left 80 rupees
Haasi (a part) of the spinning wheel broke, I spent 20 rupees on that
That left 60 rupees
Lath (another part) of the spinning wheel broke, I spent 20 rupees on that
That left 40 rupees
Your sister-in-law died, I spent 20 rupees there
That left 20 rupees
Then died your daughter and I spent 20 rupees there
There, your 100 rupees are complete!
Your 100 rupees are complete!
Your 100 rupees are complete!

YB

A poem translated from Urdu that brought the writer to tears as she shared it.

Sometimes, I feel
Sometimes, I feel enraged at my own laughter, and sometimes I want to make the whole world laugh
Sometimes, I hide my sorrows in a corner, and sometimes I want to shout them from the rooftop
Sometimes, my heart won't cry at any cost, and sometimes I want to shed tears over nothing
Sometimes, it feels nice to be free, and sometimes I want to entangle myself in a relationship
Sometimes, my own feel like strangers, and sometimes I want to make strangers my own
Sometimes, God's name doesn't touch my tongue, and sometimes he is the one I want to make up with
Sometimes, this life feels beautiful, and sometimes I want to turn away from life
Sometimes, I feel enraged at my own laughter, and sometimes I want to make the whole world laugh.

IS

Printed in Great Britain
by Amazon